W9-BWI-219

STRIP MINING

By Barbara Linde

Gareth Stevens
Publishing

Please visit our website, www.garethstevens.com. For a free color catalog of all our high-quality books, call toll free 1-800-542-2595 or fax 1-877-542-2596.

Library of Congress Cataloging-in-Publication Data

Linde, Barbara M.
Strip mining / by Barbara M. Linde.
 p. cm. — (Habitat havoc)
Includes index.
ISBN 978-1-4339-9864-5 (pbk.)
ISBN 978-1-4339-9865-2 (6-pack)
ISBN 978-1-4339-9862-1 (library binding)
1. Strip mining — Environmental aspects — United States. 2. Strip mining — Moral and ethical aspects. I. Linde, Barbara M. II. Title.
TD195.C58 L56 2014
622.292—dc23

First Edition

Published in 2014 by
Gareth Stevens Publishing
111 East 14th Street, Suite 349
New York, NY 10003

Copyright © 2014 Gareth Stevens Publishing

Designer: Andrea Davison-Bartolotta
Editor: Kristen Rajczak

Photo credits: Cover, p. 1 Andreas Bauer/E+/Getty Images; p. 4 Vera Kailova/Shutterstock.com; p. 5 Jerry Whaley/Photographer's Choice RF/Getty Images; p. 6 airphoto.gr/Shutterstock.com; p. 7 Monty Rakusen/ Cultura/Getty Images; p. 8 John W. Banagan/Photographer's Choice/Getty Images; p. 9 Photodisc/ Thinkstock; p. 11 (1) Dr. Ajay Kumar Singh/Shutterstock.com; p. 11 (2) Lee Prince/Shutterstock.com; p. 11 (3) Sarin Kunthong/Shutterstock.com; p. 11 (4) Jim Parkin/Shutterstock.com; p. 13 Ricky Carioti/The Washington Post via Getty Images; pp. 14–15, 16, 18–19 (main) American Memory/Library of Congress; p. 17 (inset) Dick Biggins/USFWS/Wikimedia Commons; p. 17 (main) iStockphoto/Thinkstock; p. 19 (inset) Frank Ramspott/ E+/Getty Images; p. 20 Robert Nickelsberg/Getty Images; p. 21 Gary Fiegehen/All Canada Photos/Getty Images; p. 23 Winfield Parks/National Geographic/Getty Images; pp. 24–25 Universal Education/Universal Images Group via Getty Images; p. 26 Jason Patrick Ross/Shutterstock.com; p. 27 Joel Sartore/National Geographic/Getty Images; p. 29 Curtis Tate/MCT via Getty Images.

Printed in the United States of America

CPSIA compliance information: Batch #CW14GS: For further information contact Gareth Stevens, New York, New York at 1-800-542-2595.

Contents

Words in the glossary appear in **bold** type the first time they are used in the text.

WHAT HAPPENED HERE?

Imagine this: You're hiking along a mountain trail. All around you, the birds are singing. You see tall, strong trees. Squirrels are climbing through the branches. Colorful flowers grow everywhere. A chipmunk runs across your path. You even see a deer nearby.

As you reach the top of the trail, you look out, hoping to see another beautiful mountaintop. But you don't. The trees and plants have been ripped out. There's a huge gash in the ground. Noisy machines are scraping and digging. Dust fills the air. You have just seen your first strip mine.

A Bit About Mining

Many of the **minerals**, **fossil fuels**, and metals we use are buried in the ground. They're found in underground **deposits**. Mining takes these raw materials out of the ground. Mining is also used to remove gravel, sand, and rocks. People use the mined materials for fuel, building, and even jewelry!

active mine

Mines can be found in many countries worldwide.

HABITATS ARE HOMES

A habitat is a place where a plant or animal lives and grows. There are many kinds of habitats. A forest can be a habitat for many things. Is there a beehive hanging from a tree? Perhaps a snake has a den in the ground. Trees, bushes, and flowers have habitats in the forest.

You have a habitat, too. It includes the city or town you live in, your neighborhood, and your backyard!

Habitats may be ruined or harmed by pollution that comes from many different sources and activities. Strip mining is one danger a habitat can face.

Habitat Loss

When habitats are lost, whether because of natural or human-led activities, animals struggle. Some may be able to move to other habitats and adapt to new surroundings. Other animals can only live in one place. If their habitat is lost, the whole animal group may die out.

coal mine

Human actions cause many of the problems in habitats around the world today.

WHAT IS STRIP MINING?

There are two main types of mining: underground and surface mining. In underground mines, large machines dig holes and tunnels far into the ground. Miners work underground, digging out the materials. Raw materials that are deeper than 800 feet (244 m) are taken out by underground mining.

Strip mining is a type of surface mining. It's used to collect minerals and fossil fuels found at depths shallower than 800 feet. All the mining is done in strips by machines and explosives. Coal deposits, called seams, are often taken out by strip mining.

Super Pit gold mine

The Super Pit Mine

The Fimiston, or Super Pit, is the largest open-pit gold mine in Western Australia. An open-pit mine is another kind of surface mine. The Super Pit is about 2.2 miles (3.5 km) long, 0.9 mile (1.5 km) wide, and 1,181 feet (360 m) deep. Since work goes on 24 hours a day, it could more than double in size quickly.

Bulldozers and huge machines called draglines and wheel loaders are used in strip mining.

Strip mining for coal has several steps:

1. Surface soil, rocks, and plants, called **overburden**, are taken away and stored in a nearby valley or piled up near the mine.

2. The layer of rocks above the coal seam is drilled away or blasted apart. These rocks are stored with the other materials.

3. Now the deposits of coal are blasted apart. Then, the coal is taken by truck to a processing plant.

4. Reclamation begins. This means that the land is made to look roughly like it did before. Soil and overburden are returned, and new trees and plants are put in place.

Reclamation Is the Law!

The Surface Mining Control and Reclamation Act of 1977 says all land used for surface mining must be reclaimed. It has to be returned to the same as or better condition than it was before mining began. The US government monitors these efforts and works with mining companies to make the land useful again. So far, millions of acres of land have been reclaimed.

1

overburden
piles

2

coal seam

3

4

Strip mining works best in flatter
areas with a thin overburden.

IS STRIP MINING HARMFUL?

Strip mining is a **controversial** topic. This chart shows the basic arguments made for and against strip mining in the United States. The following chapters will help you decide which side you're on!

The Pros and Cons of Strip Mining

pro	con
• People need mined materials for fuel and other things.	• Mining harms the **environment**, as well as the people and wildlife near mines.
• Laws have been put in place to make mining practices safer for miners and surrounding habitats.	• Companies don't always follow the laws.
• Mining creates many jobs.	• Mining can be a dangerous job.
• Strip mining only occurs for a short time.	• Reclamation efforts aren't always successful.
• Companies are required by law to reclaim the land.	• The effects of mining can last a long time.

Protestors against strip mining in the Appalachian Mountains crowd outside the White House in Washington, DC, in 2010.

Greenpeace

Greenpeace works in countries around the world to stop actions harming the environment. Those in the group actively oppose strip mining. They plan protests and talks to teach people about the dangers. Greenpeace also tries to work with members of Congress to pass stricter laws for mining companies.

SPOILED SOIL

Soil has small living things and **nutrients** in it. These help plants grow. When soil is dug up at a strip mine, the living things may be killed. The soil is often mixed with overburden while mining occurs. Over time, the nutrients in it can be lost. When the soil and overburden mixture is put back during reclamation, new plants may not be able to grow in it.

Mining can also poison the soil with toxins from mining waste. Once these are in the soil, they may stay for a long time. This is especially worrisome in the Midwest, where strip mines are being reclaimed for farmland.

Western Woes

The western United States has a dry climate. The native plants are able to live without much water. However, because it's sometimes cheaper, mining companies may use nonnative plants during the reclaiming process. These may not grow as well. If their roots don't hold, then **erosion** may take place. Native animals might not like eating the strange plants, either.

Whether reclamation works often depends on how healthy the soil is.

WATER WORRIES

The raw materials in mines often have toxins in them that can leak into the groundwater or streams, poisoning them. If the water turns murky brown, red, or another color, it's easy to notice the pollution. Still, many toxins are colorless. They mix with the water, but no one knows they're there—that is, until someone sees dead fish floating on the water's surface.

Coal companies try to keep their waste out of the groundwater. But, accidents have happened. So, water near strip mines has to be closely monitored to make sure it's up to the standards set by the Clean Water Act.

The Buffalo Creek Disaster

The Pittston Coal Company began dumping mine waste into Buffalo Creek in West Virginia in 1957. They built dams to keep a mix of toxic coal dust and other pollutants out of the water beyond. In February 1972, heavy rains caused the dams to burst, and the toxic sludge flowed out. Towns flooded, 125 people died, and over 1,000 people were hurt.

Buffalo Creek memorial

The Cumberland darter and blackside dace are two freshwater fish with already low populations. Environmental groups in Tennessee worry that the building of a nearby strip mine will cause too much pollution for these fish to survive.

blackside dace

MOUNTAINTOP MISERY

Strip mining sometimes removes the whole top of a mountain! It destroys plants and animals while doing so. The overburden is dumped into nearby valleys, clogging up streams and keeping fish and other animals from **migrating**. The overburden may be toxic, too, so it poisons the ground and water it touches.

Coal companies say that mountaintop removal is the quickest and cheapest way to reach coal seams. However, it may remove 500 to 800 feet (152 to 244 m) of mountaintop that can't be replaced. Often, the new, flat top can't be reclaimed or reused. The beauty of the area is also ruined.

Concerns in Appalachia

Coal mining has been a way of life in the Appalachian Mountains since the 1700s. Mountaintop mining is used a lot there now. This upsets many people who live there. They're unhappy the land isn't always reclaimed. Mountaintop mining uses a lot of large machinery instead of miners. So, many miners are losing their jobs.

Mountaintop removal has been occurring since the 1970s, mostly in Tennessee, West Virginia, Virginia, and Kentucky.

Appalachian Mountains

19

NOT-SO-FRESH AIR

Digging at a mine and mining trucks driving on unpaved roads create a lot of dust. Coal companies try to cut down on the dust by spraying the roads with water and using dust collection systems on their drills, but what escapes still pollutes the air.

Toxic gases can't be seen, but they also get into the air. Methane is one toxic gas that may enter the air because of coal mining. It forms underground with coal over millions of years. Scientists have found methane to be a **greenhouse gas**, so companies try to capture it and use it for energy instead of letting it seep into the air.

Buckskin Coal Mine in Gillette, Wyoming

Noise pollution from a mine can be heard for miles. Trucks and other machines have huge, noisy engines. The booms from an explosion can be deafening.

Coal Fires

Lightning and forest fires can cause coal fires, but they most commonly start with mining accidents. Aboveground and belowground fires may go on for hundreds of years! The air fills with thick, toxic smoke that contains greenhouse gases. The ground and air near the fire get superhot. Water and soil are poisoned. Living things may get hurt, sick, or even die.

OTHER PROBLEMS

Many times, people who live close to a mine get sick. The toxins from overburden and mining materials build up in their bodies as they drink poisoned water or breathe in poisonous gases. This causes heart, lung, and kidney diseases, as well as cancers.

Thousands of miners around the world die each year in mine accidents, too. Falling rocks, mine collapses, and accidents with heavy machinery killed more than 4,700 people in Chinese coal mines in 2006 alone.

Miners may get a serious disease called black lung and have to stop working. Usually, lungs are soft and squishy. Coal dust makes them hard so air can't move in and out.

Protests in Phulbari, Bangladesh

People in Phulbari, Bangladesh, have been protesting a proposed open-pit coal mine since 2006. The mine would destroy 100 villages and acres of rich farmland. They believe the mine wastes would poison or dry up their wells. Over 200,000 people would have to move. In 2012, those against the project asked the government to ban it.

Breathing in coal dust harms miners' lungs. About 1,200 people in the United States die from the disease called black lung every year.

Strip mining often destroys parts of forests. This harms the whole forest, and it looks bad. Imagine driving along a mountain road and seeing huge gaps in the trees. Reclamation includes planting new trees, but it may take hundreds of years for a tree to fully grow. Even when trees are replanted, a new forest will grow slowly. And that's if the trees grow at all!

Worldwide Damage

According to a Greenpeace study, coal mining has damaged or destroyed almost 6 million acres (2.4 million ha) of land in the United States and 8 million acres (3.2 million ha) in China. Mining for coal, gold, copper, and other materials has also destroyed land in South Africa, India, Peru, Russia, Spain, and many other countries.

Since the toxins from overburden and mine waste tend to stay in the soil for a long time, it's possible that plants won't grow in reclaimed areas. Or, new kinds of plants will grow. Either way, the habitat has been changed, perhaps for the worse.

This used to be a beautiful forest, but a strip mine changed this habitat for good.

When the plant cover is stripped away, plant-eating animals lose their food. Some may die, while others move. If they move to an area that has many other animals, there may not be enough food. Birds lose their homes when the trees are cut down. Eggs or baby birds in nests often die.

Just as toxins from the overburden and other materials poison people, they also poison fish and other animals living in water near a mining site. The soil and overburden fill in streams, too. In Appalachia, this is a real problem for salamanders. Many have died because their habitats disappear when strip mining begins.

red salamander

Battle for the Bats

When a new mine is being built, the effects it would have on local animal populations are considered. In Harrisburg, Illinois, environmental groups raised concerns that a proposed strip mine in part of the Shawnee National Forest would harm already low numbers of bats in the area. This worry has delayed the building of the mine.

This photograph shows one of many surface coal mines in the Powder River Basin in Wyoming. People living near that area have asked the government to slow coal production and consider ongoing environmental problems.

NEW HOMES FROM OLD MINES

In 1989, the Ohio Power Company gave almost 10,000 acres (4,050 ha) of reclaimed strip mine land to a group of zoos. The zoos turned the land into an animal **preserve** called The Wilds! Now, African animals such as giraffes and zebras roam the grassy plains.

Poplar Gap Park in Virginia opened in 2001, and you'd never know it sits on top of an old strip mine. Birds sing and wildlife thrive in the healthy forest.

These successes show that with careful reclamation efforts, old strip mines can be healthy habitats again. However, the original destruction caused by strip mining is still a troubling and often controversial topic.

Good News!

Animals are doing well at the Powder River Basin reclaimed coal mine in Gillette, Wyoming. Rabbits, foxes, squirrels, deer, and many other forest animals live on the land. Hawks, golden eagles, and other birds fly through the skies. No hunting is allowed, so the animals are safe there.

When strip mines are reclaimed properly, they can be beautiful places to visit.

Glossary

controversial: having to do with controversy, or a discussion that has different sides arguing their views

deposit: an amount of a mineral in the ground that built up over a period of time

environment: the natural world in which a plant or animal lives

erosion: the act of wearing away by wind or water

fossil fuel: matter formed over millions of years from plant and animal remains that is burned for power

greenhouse gas: a gas that rises into the atmosphere and doesn't allow heat to escape

migrate: to move to warmer or colder places for a season

mineral: matter in the ground that forms rocks

nutrient: something a living thing needs to grow and stay alive

overburden: the plants, soil, and rocks that are removed from over a mineral deposit

preserve: a place set aside for animals and plants

For More Information

Books

Orme, Helen. *Habitat Destruction.* New York, NY: Bearport Publishing, 2009.

Parks, Peggy J. *Coal Power.* San Diego, CA: ReferencePoint Press, 2011.

Websites

Mining Impacts: Greenpeace International
www.greenpeace.org/international/en/campaigns/climate-change/coal/Mining-impacts/
Read about strip mining from the point of view of an environmental group. Learn how strip mining damages the land and how that land may be saved.

Razing Appalachia
www.pbs.org/independentlens/razingappalachia/mtop.html
Learn more about mountaintop removal in the Appalachian Mountains and the impact of coal energy production on the environment.

Index